I am Revel Martin, author of the book *Streams of Poetic Proverbs*, published by Rose Dog Books. I live in the island country of Trinidad and Tobago in the West Indies. I am a lawman with a wife and three children. I love stargazing, cricket and writing stories.

To the spirit of God

Revel Martin

BEFORE HOPE DIES

AUSTIN MACAULEY PUBLISHERS™
LONDON · CAMBRIDGE · NEW YORK · SHARJAH

Copyright © Revel Martin 2024

The right of Revel Martin to be identified as author of this work has been asserted by the author in accordance with sections 77 and 78 of the Copyright, Designs and Patents Act 1988.

All rights reserved. No part of this publication may be reproduced, stored in a retrieval system, or transmitted in any form or by any means, electronic, mechanical, photocopying, recording, or otherwise, without the prior permission of the publishers.

Any person who commits any unauthorised act in relation to this publication may be liable to criminal prosecution and civil claims for damages.

A CIP catalogue record for this title is available from the British Library.

ISBN 9781035800506 (Paperback)
ISBN 9781035800513 (ePub e-book)

www.austinmacauley.com

First Published 2024
Austin Macauley Publishers Ltd®
1 Canada Square
Canary Wharf
London
E14 5AA

To my wife, Gillian, my children and my niece, Tabeel.

Foreword

I have enclosed, for your consideration, the manuscript for my book titled, *Before Hope Dies*. A book of general collection of poems or literature – I would like to say part fiction, part non-fiction – put together into one book with meter style, humour and with a serious intensity. It is taken from the backdrop of what is happening in the world today, both past and present. As a little boy, growing up, you hear stories that the world is going to end. It did not happen then, but now it's almost too familiar. Along the way, you encounter problems, and when dealt correctly, you learn from it. You become stronger by it so that you can help someone else, who is also facing similar trials. There are many questions that need answers, and it is not in the gun or in the war. Times are getting difficult. This book is a journey of emotions; that's what poets do. This book is comprehensive and portrays life in a perplex way, which is evident in these poems: *Hidden Spirit* and *There Is Going to Come a Time* and *Before Hope Dies.* I do hope you enjoy this book.

Yours respectfully,
Revel Martin

Poetry

Has the world lost its touch on poetry?
I hope not, for that will be a tragedy
Why can't we remember the stories?
It's all in our history
Philosophy, can this be
That philosophy has taken over poetry?
Then where would our poets be
Who filled our hearts with their symphonies?
Symphonies of words captured
As we write our compositions
And played it to our audience
Who remembered the harmony
Of this sweet poetry

Voices Beckoning

The Journey to where we are going
Can often be misleading, you get my drift?
Because there are many voices out there
And the voices are crying out "follow I"
Who is this "I" that we should follow?
For we have viewed the manner
In which we did not know better
That these voices were not of a true nature.
Why will so many voices call out at the same time?
Yes, to drown out the only one true voice
Which speaks of better things
Which has the power to demonstrate great things
But these other voices are a travesty
For they used wealth or mind control to subdue us
And yet we cannot break free
The lies are too much of a lie to believe that it's a lie
Have the voices so persuaded us
That we cannot see beyond the mask?
God help us.
Yes, the voices that we are compelled to hear
Is beckoning, "look I am your saviour".
If our minds serve us well
We were forewarned about these Antichrists
And I am not following, even if it causes me my life
I have pulled out myself from the crowd
That follow these voices on a journey, which can only mean death
Now I feel the absolute loneliness
Which the voices find necessary to buffet me
The images that were once behind the voices were lambs
But now, it's that of a sinister
Ready to kill my body for I know too much.
Who can save me from the terror of these voices?
Oh, it was a mistake to give my heart to them
And now they are demanding loyalty

But I will not give in.
And for this, I was beheaded
Now I, the poet, remain to testify that my friend
Is now with the king, whose voice we heard to the end.

The Question Why

Why is my life this way? I will like to know
What did I do to deserve such sadness?
Who is this being? Why is he not helping?
Is he the author of my suffering?
Then I will like to know why
Oh, he is somewhere up in the sky
Does he know that I am hurting
And that I need some answers?
When I look around, I can see others smiling
Things are good with them, unless they are pretending
Life can be a funny thing, you see
I did not have a choice
I did not understand why my life was going through this
Experiences of loneliness, experiencing hardship
Being called all sorts of names by my loved ones
Why? Was I not a good child?
I was obedient to my parents
Oh, it had to be the devil, who else?
For he is that sinner from the beginning of creation.
I want happiness, for that is all I ever wanted
For I know now, why
The devil was trying to keep me from becoming a child of God
That I will blame God for all my misdeeds
And because I now know why
I give God thanks for the victory in Jesus

Shut Up Against That Day

I dread the day that is at hand
Who knows what I am talking about?
It was always inside of me
And now, I must face the agony
It is that time again, for I must leave my children
Oh how I cried, seeing that life must go on
They were loaned to me by God Almighty
On my knees I said, "Lord, keep them"
On my knees I said, "Lord, thy will be done"
As I lay my hands, be blessed my children
Love Poet

On the Wings of the Morning

Come and see what I see
Is your imagination as wild as mine?
Then lift up your eyes to the hills
Do not be afraid, for you will not be hurt
As you take the wings of an eagle
And soar on the morning breath
Viewing all the wonders of valleys and mountains
A sight for sore eyes.
All this I will give you and more
A foretaste of what has been hidden
And what has not yet been spoken of until now
This is your inheritance
I have kept it for you since from the beginning
While you were in your mother's womb
A father ought to lay up treasures for his children,
Children
Ah, chariots of fire, you have come for me at last
Where you'll take me into my treasures
Where I'll be in the bosom of Abraham
Looking down at my sons
On the wings of the morning

Have You Listened to the Quietness?

In a lifetime, if you are not aware
Your life could slip away right from under you
Because you were too preoccupied
That you left without giving thanks
And now, pride has filled your heart
What is the matter?
Can you not remember your humble beginning?
That it was me who gave you the wisdom
And power to get wealth
Well, are you so reluctant
That you cannot resist the path you are on?
Which leads to your downfall?
Are you so blind to everything
That I allowed to come your way?
To shake you up a little bit?
By the way, have you listened to the quietness?
It's scary, ain't it?
Be it may, that's your conscience
It has been sheared by a hot iron
And now you are doing everything that is against me
But I am able to bring you back
If you just simply repent
And listen to your quietness
It might save you from falling from grace.
For this is my plea,
Love, Jesus

Consciously Alarm

As one who likes to observe
And understand the things that he should
For not everything is visible
For not everyone tells the truth
And you got to know who you are dealing with
For life is full of characters
And we come across them frequently
Because, it's a real world.
And I'm consciously alarmed of the fact
That not all hearts are pure.
So, I got burnt by false pretence
For not everyone is genuine
And because of these events in my life,
I'm consciously alarmed, not taking the chance,
With wolves in sheep's clothing.

You Can Run but You Cannot Hide

Can you ever imagine that the only way you can breathe
Is when the cares of this life are behind you?
For you got yourself entangled with a lifestyle
That was never meant for you
But you went ahead anyway
And now! You're running away from your mistakes
Who would have thought that you will get away from the trouble
You Caused?
Knowing that your sins will surely find you out
And no matter how far you run, you just cannot simply hide
For you will remember, it does not pay to do evil
And pretend not, you would not reach far by avoiding
Your problems
So, be a man, and live up to your actions
For it is impossible to run and hide at the same time

Life

Life is not what it seems
Not always what you intended it to be
Life, I though it to be easy
But quite the contrary.
It turned out to be most crazy.
People with their attitudes and problems
Not knowing how to solve them
Life with its many difficulties
Please! Who has the remedy?
I went to a doctor.
He prescribed me a lawyer
The lawyer was too busy to handle my life's anxiety.
So, I went on the streets
To see if there was any security.
None, but only misery.
Then I was on the run,
Thinking life was going to strike me down
Not so, not so as I thought
It's only here to make me strong.
And with that, I embraced life
No more to strife, thank God, who gives life.

Unsettled

I long for some relaxation
But I wonder if I am asking for too much
There is a saying that there is no rest for the wicked
But I am not wicked
So how come I am not settled?
Unsettled because of the wrong choices
That can make your life miserable.
Why, I ask myself, was I born to be unsettled?
Ok.
The word seems frequent
That I am so much desirous for a change
That after I suffered a while, I can be settled.

Running with the Equine

Would you think for a moment
And see how the story would unfold?
Then go through it and see with me
I am thinking about purpose
And sticking to what I have started
I am thinking about determination
As they say, sticking to the guns
Is what this is all about?
I am thinking about trying out my ideas
And not bowing down to failures
Though I fall, I shall arise again
For nothing comes easy, do you understand my poetry?
I am thinking about running with the equine
For they are the ones that beat us to it
Is it because of their monies
Or are they just born geniuses?
While the system is in their hands
Do you see the picture I am painting?
Should I make it simpler?
You cannot let any man despise your youth
For the potentials that is inside of you
So then run with the equine, and beat them to it
For young men are strong
And there is a vision to it all
So tuck in that gut and run.

How Might I Capture the Firmament

One day I was searching for an adventure
But nothing seemed daring enough
Like the Sahara Desert or Mount Everest
And I was bored, nothing for the sake of fun
Until one day I was gazing at the evening sky
Watching how beautiful it looked
As the sun sets over the horizon
That I wondered, I can only capture
This firmament in its glory
And place it among my collections
Then I would have done well
To be the only adventurer
With the firmament in his possessions
But look at the publicity
I can see it now
If I could only capture the firmament
Then I can do whatever I determine
For the firmament will be in my collections.
Then I thought within myself
What will be greater
The firmament or the creator?
For if I have Him, then I will have unlimited power.
But Folks! Surprising enough
That's what caused Satan's down fall
Though I reach for the firmament
It will be only in amazement
For the creator is greatly to be feared
And how may I capture the firmament?
I cannot, not in the way I imagine
But with my heart and soul
Is the firmament captured

The End

Before Hope Dies

I rush to recover the last remains of hope
But it was difficult: the emotions, the thoughts
As I stop to sob, it was too much for me to comprehend
The seriousness, the catastrophe
Of this loss brought on me
That I went around discreetly
Not letting my comrades know
That without hope
We are people, most miserable
They heard me speak of hope in much patience
That even they themselves knew
That hope makes not ashamed
For the love it brings in living
Especially in a world of tribulation
That I promised myself that I will tell no one
Even though those were his words
And my comrades, and the world by extension
Saw me live hope in much affliction
So encouraging them to live on unto the end
Which I thank God, I did not tell.

Kings and Queens

World order, world populations
World's religion, world crisis
Colonialism, peace and blunderbuss
Gathering its slow victims, as they try
Crossing the river of asylum
No hope today, but tomorrow is hope enough
To keep this word resounding
"One day, one day"

Pirates

Amongst the parched bones I lay
Disfigured, oh, but in a good way
To elude my captures
Who wanted my head, they say
It's a command from the king
So give up your self today
This was their proclamation
As I heard it, lying there between the skeletons
My only hope for survival
Is the silence of these frame work
Bones of heroes, but I will not be joining them today
For I must live to tell the tale
Of how I eluded the king of Spain.

A Thing of the Past

When did it all end
The good times?
And as the world moves into the twenty-first century
All I have left is memories
Where you could have left your house open
And you did not have to worry about thieves breaking in
A thing of the past is when we loved our neighbours as ourselves
Sharing the produce of our gardens
Cassava, eddoes, and plantain, and yes, pumpkins
And now we have to hire security against
Praedial larceny.
Time has really changed
A thing of the past.
I could not have gone out
With a girl, unless I saw her father first
And pleaded with him, that I will have her home by ten
A thing of the past, as I remember
Living in my house in St Croix Trinidad
My daddy was a strict man, my mother quiet
My community not how it was
I guess the past is best left behind
But then, what kind of a future we will have?

Perils

Where to begin, at the end or at the beginning
Or at the middle?
But what I am about to say just happened
With no beginning or an end.
Dead and gone into the after life
Seeing creatures I cannot describe
Gross darkness encamped around me
Oh the rewards for my misdeeds.
What I will do for life again
To walk amongst the living
Too late, too late is the cry
Demons howl my name out loud
They laugh and say, you had your chance
And now you are in peril of eternal damnation
Earthly perils cannot be compared to Hell's perils
And this is my sentence, Oh to the horror of men,
Perils.

Who Influencing Who

I am amazed to see
And I am yet to come to terms
With what frightens me
This journal is not for the faintish or weak of heart
But if they decide to read this poem
Let him or her pray
For the path that I have chosen has it consequences
Blinded and misleading, deceived are we
And on top of that, is our body with its infirmities
Stress, frustration, and anxieties
But the stronger of these is likely to be unforgiveness.
I am in Hell,
A place people said did not exist
How could I be this foolish
To allow this world to influence me?
The road I have taken seemed right
But the end there of was death
I allowed my friends to persuade me
When you lived by the sword, you will perish by the sword
Why did I ever listen?
Forsaking the advice of my parents
And now my blood is crying out
From the place where the worms die not
I can hear Satan saying, you are mine
But he looks familiar, like unto the son of man
So adding to my afflictions
For all were created in his likeness and image
That's why his influence is a disguise
So hiding behind the light
For Satan is not Christ, and could never be
My parents warned me about the path that I was on
And I chose my friends over them
But I regret the moment when I said I hated Christ
Oh, I wish I could take that back
I cried and I cried ah, ah, ah, with such a groan

But my tears mean nothing in a place such as hell
Fire, fire all around me.
Help, help, I am in agony
At one time I did hear a God-fearing man say something
About this place, to some extent
But I thought he was lying, and that was my mistake.
You know the worse thing about this?
I can see paradise afar off
And it's beautiful there, believe me, it's real
Oh what a waste of life that is mine
And the countless others
To the young people who walk amongst the living
Stop and think
For you would not be given another chance
When you come to this place called Hell
Who Influencing who.

Distant Dreams

It's funny how dreams come true
To be a Nelson Mandela was never imagined
But yet it happened
Was it in my subconscious? I really can't say
But I am living in a palace
Carrying out my presidential duties
As a boy I never imagined
That I'd see my manhood
Through the eyes of a prison
Locked up for life
I never thought I'd feel
The warmth of a woman
To make love to her, only as a man can
And yes, I do have my strength
Distant dreams fulfilled
I am glad I did not give in
To the pressures of fellow inmates
Look at me now
I am governing a whole country
Distant dreams really do come true
President Nelson Mandela

Crystal Lake

Growing up, I always used to hear about this Crystal Lake.
But never did I believe it existed
Until I stumbled on it.
That this Crystal Lake was really in a place
Beyond our human imagination
That I thought it to be a myth, but I guess not
And there it was, right before my eyes
This Crystal Lake, so peaceful as it was beautiful
And I went closer to see
If it was really what people said it would be
That this Crystal Lake healed them of all their mental disabilities.
And I kept looking at it, this Crystal Lake
Wondering if I'll become one with it
For it did take my breath away.
The scenery was glorious
That this place must be in the Garden of Eden
As I was in my moment, a woman came and said,
"Sir, this museum is closing this minute"
I lost my vision as I was distracted
And now I may not regain it.
That this Crystal Lake was a portrait
Wonderfully constructed to capture
The imagination of the onlooker's wow.

What Do You Hear at the Earth Surface?

One day I was asked this question by my professor
We were studying the formation of the earth's crust
And he asked me this,
What do you hear at the earth surfaces?
Strange question
I said what, what do I hear at the earth surface.
"Sir," I said, "that is not part of the study"
So I wonder if too much learning has made him crazy
Has my professor gone superstitious on me?
For he is beginning to frighten me
Where does he come up with these alluded questions?
And my professor was staring at me straight in my eyes
Eyeball to eyeball, as if to expect an answer
Then I began to somewhat choke on my saliva
He laughed, my professor, putting me in an awkward position
"Anything yet, Bovel?"
"Yes, but I wonder if to say it."
"Well, go ahead," replied my professor
"What I am hearing at the surface is the cry of men
How their blood had been spilled
And the earth is crying out their anguish
Anguish for justice
I don't know how I am hearing it
But it's coming to me loud and clear"
The professor, looking at me
Wondering if I am the crazy one
"That is enough study for today, Bovel
I'll go home and think on what you have said
For this might be another controversial study
What do you hear at the earth surface, interesting."

Time

They said time flies when you are having fun
But you ever stop to think why
They said time waits on no man
I wonder why, so with this in mind
I went to time and said
Time, could I have a minute of your time?
He said, no chance, and I said
It would only be for a few seconds
I, time, know the questions you want to ask
Why don't I wait on man
Especially when he's having fun?
But if I do that, what do you think will be my position?
There would be no equilibrium
And there would be no given time for the sun to rise
Or for the moon to shine in the night sky
So my answer to you is no
I will not wait on man.
Man has been given a stipulate time
That's me to do his duty
And your duties are to give God the glory
And do the work that is necessary
So that at the end of time, "me"
You will all live with God in eternity.

Hidden Spirts

Alone for me again
As I think the strangest things
Locked up in a prison
Where I can only look through a barred glass window
How I dreamt for the day
When my spirit would be free
From these hidden mind fields
I envy those that walk free
With their secrets all hidden
But I was not fortunate
Because I took it on
And now I have to be restrained
Oh how I wish I did not
But something propelled me to
And now they say I am crazy
Hidden spirits are my worst enemy

In the Still of the Night

I was in the midst of my own turmoil
And I the poet needed some time out
So I resorted to when the lights were off
Then I went to my window and gazed outside
It was in the still of the night
When my mind reflected on the pressures I was having
That I took a deep breath and started talking to myself
Why is this happening to me?
And what have I done wrong? I pondered
Is it that I am weak?
The feelings over powering me
In the still of the night
You can really decide whether you'll live or die
It's a fact that demons will surely play with your mind
For it's the habitation they like
So be warned,
That your answers come to you in the light.

Memoirs

There is so much a poet can say
But would life allow him the time to say it?
For as life is immortal, my body is of the dust
And from whence it must return
I have lived my life to the likes and dislikes of people
Who to please, I am not sure.
Events that make our world unstable
For you got one on each side, saying
He has the answer
And another one on that side, he has the solution
And another one proclaiming
I do not know, but I'm willing to try anything
We have put our trust in idiots
Who just take us for a ride
People without a vision perish
So we really cannot hold unto broken promises
That's how I have seen my years
And now I must depart
Testimonies of what I have seen and heard,
Memoirs, I leave with you.

Fathom This

So many of us like to see a world complete with peace
Where mankind can live in harmony
And do you see the constant upheavals?
A world that is trying to cope with the many demands
Of striving nations
But the nations are making it difficult
That they cannot fathom their own conflicts
So the world is suffering
Spiritual leaders appointed by men
Giving wrong advice
Watch, do you see any difference?
No, only pain and misery
But can we truly fathom this present evil?
No, but we should not fight amongst each other
Instead, let us focus our attention
On bringing down the barriers that discriminate
Each from the other
For there is only one human race
Even though we are separated by the colour of our skin
But hey, we do have the same coloured blood.

Love Is Colour Blind

I tried my best at "love"
But she never seems interested in what I'm offering
No catch to my persistence
For "love" is one that should be given freely
If proven trustworthy.
What the heck! It's love I long for
And you shouldn't give up until you find it
For "love" can be in the strangest of places
But love, I must distinctively know
For there is love of a white woman,
And also of a black woman, but which one
I shouldn't rather
And what does it matter if love
Loves me from the flesh of a white
Should I be denied? For love is colour-blind.

There's Going to Come a Time

There's going to come a time
Where Christians will not endure sound doctrine
There's going to come a time
Where men's hearts will fail them because of fear
Oh, it's the things that are coming upon the earth
That will excite them
Where men's hearts will be wax cold
As if that is not happening already
And it's love that makes the world go around
Then how come we are not patient with each other?
Man who has built weapons of mass destruction.
There's going to come a time
Where this man who knows to do wickedly
Will plunge the world into total chaos through flattery.
There's going to come a time
Where the world as we know it
Will be no more, as our children will no more run free
Where democracy will have no meaning
Where the world will be in absolute darkness
And when that time shall come
It will be the end of us all.

The Moving of the Tide

How I imagine if there was some kind of soundness
To the uneasiness I am feeling
Is it all to the unexpected
And where do I fit in all of this?
Can you see what's dawning?
And is it to the favour of mankind?
If yes, then we have nothing to fear then
But if not, then we cannot allow it
It's about this world order
And this new age power
Where this man who understands dark sentences
Will arise from
And the law makers who are moving to this tide
To a pending disaster
Oh, how I wish I was not born
For who shall stop him
The course is already set
And who is not aware
Shall be swept away by the moving of the tide
One government, one religion, one world order.

Hell Is Real

Simple, simple. I write my verse
No big words, just in the language of my native birth
Brown coloured and all, but yet I found myself
A thousand miles from home
Keeping the letters of stories told
Of myths and legends, a custom preserved
Chains that tells me that I am going nowhere soon
A woman given, to further their industry
Seeds auction the moment wean,
This place, Hell is real

Sorrowful

There are some thoughts in my head
That I can feel in my loins
Yes, and it may not be easy to explain
It is when sorrow becomes so great
That my mind needs to channel it
And that's where my loins come in
Funny, ain't it? But it's true.
And if one of your fingers suffer
It's evident that your whole body suffers with it
Well, it's the law of the body
You suffer, I suffer
You rejoice, I rejoice
That the members of the body are fitly joined
So when the thoughts of my head become too much
It's when my loins steps in
For I am thinking that my life is nothing but a flower
Which is today, and tomorrow it withers away.

Equinox

It's that time of the year
No, it's not Christmas
It has nothing to do with jingle bell all the way
But it's that time when light and darkness are equal in
length, I never knew this.
The night comes where no man can work
Oh man! What you do, do it fast
For the day is almost pass
So you had your time to shine
To do good under the sun
Where there were times for everything
A time to be born, to die, to plant, to reap
That which was planted, a time to kill, to heal
To break down, to build up, to weep, to laugh
To mourn, to dance, to embrace, to refrain from embracing
To get, to lose, to keep, to cast away, to love, to hate
To go to war, and to have peace
All this in the boundaries of the day
And a full day had its length
And now the darkness shall cover the earth
Oh how I wish that length can be shortened
For the elect sake, where children would be
Making children, and bombs exploding
No peace, but sudden destruction.
I have lived my full length which is three score and ten
It's this generation to catch
My children, oh my God, Lord, help them
As they face this equinox of darkness.

The Trial of This Time

Oh, it's the year twenty twenty-one
And what's the prediction
For one who wants to be successful
Without getting into trouble?
Don't come to me and say you can sell drugs
I do not want to get into an altercation with the law
What about organizing a big robbery?
The banks has the money.
Look, I want to be an upstanding citizen.
Hear this, we are a part of a secret society
And we follow the tradition of the Nazis
No way! For when I'm in that, the hate alone will
Consume me
Now, if you sell your body,
There is a lot of guys who will love you
What is this at all, and what is the world coming to?
The pleasure of a woman is far enjoyable than a man
How could you come to me with that?
I know! We can smuggle arms into countries
Terrorist are paying big money for this
You want me to be an outlaw?
But not so at all
If you want to be successful, this is the way to go
No fool. What about doing what is right
And following the teachings of our elders?
That it does not pay to live by the sword
Ok! If that's your decision, I will leave you
To follow your part. So, this is goodbye
Trials is to make the best out of us, so be smart.

A Shew of Might

I understand that there is a shew of might in all of us
That needs to be channelled in some way or the other
But because of evil persuasiveness
Much of our strength has been diverted,
Diverted from the common good, where all are equal
For we used our shew of might to separate ourselves
From the others,
Putting up racial barriers
Like apartheid
Or the crackdown in Tiananmen square "China"
Not forgetting boko Haram "Nigeria"
Where our shew of might was used for dominating others
So, there is a shew of might taking place between good and evil
And this shew of might has been going on for centuries
Where we have been caught in the cross fire
Now where is your strength being channelled?
Is it to the fuel of evil?
I hope you know what you are doing
Or is it to the fuel of good?
If so, then there is hope for your children
And please, let your shew of might help each other.

Epilogue

This is an episode, a series of events of epic proportions
A brown coloured man is president of Uncle Sam.
I ask how this thing is going to play out.
Should I open my eyes, keep it shut?
A coloured man is commander and chief
Of the most powerful nation on the earth
Wow! Look at that, it was South Africa
Now America, black men in power
But this is no story or a play or make-believe
For this event did actually happen in my day
And it has become stories and plays
So that our children can see history in the making
What a time to be living in
Historians have their plate full
Even theologian preaching, oh, it's written in the word
Prophecies unfold
And one who has seen it all, my epilogue
Words written, that great men come in different shades.

My Stories or Not

What is it about these stories that's intriguing?
It's a little of me, and poetry
And it's appealing because of its simplicity
That I write my stories in the simplicity of poetry
So the young and old can read my verse.
I am not all that loud
And I can hold my end in a conversation
As I was brought upright by living a simple life
Always quiet, I hate violence
For the pain and grief it brings
People driven by their emotions
That at times you just have to stay far, far, far away
Is there no love in this world?
A world that we are born into
That the only way out is through death
Another problem, "death"
My dad used to say, It's a dog-eat-dog world out there
And how to protect our children
Who were born innocent up to eight years
And no matter how we educate them
Somebody might come along and kill them, God forbid
This is the world we live in
These are the stories that be my stories or not
And please love yourself, your fellow men
And live to the upliftment of others, thanks.

Third World

We have been branded third world
Asia, South and Central America, and Africa
And bet your bottom dollar
The West Indies is somewhere in the middle
Who told us that we are third world?
Poor or developing is what it means
And who told you that I am not developed?
Poor because I cannot afford the basic things?
How come I am driving the best cars?
Living in a big house?
That I am third world?
My life does not show this
My relationship with God tells me different
Third world, I do not know where the hell that came
From?
And if you ask me, that is total nonsense
And we accept it, them who do not know better
But I will tell it by the way I live
So, no one is going to subject me to a word
Or a statement that says
That I am third world.

Exploring

I set out on a part that is life
I long to find out who I am
So I came among many junctions that
Had an arrow pointing to a way that may seem right
But the end of that is death.
So, I heard a lot of philosophers say
That I am a guru or a god,
Then how come I am not convinced?
Still not satisfied with their theories and logic
I hope to find out what is my true existence.
Why me, what is my purpose amongst the races?
To be a rocket scientist, or a garbage collector
Or to be a mercenary? Ah! Not me.
Exploring the many facets of life
I came to this one where I will serve God
Now this ends the uneasiness in my soul
That I am exploring my newfound love.

Criticism

I will like this day to be one without criticism
As I get to the point, not all can take talk
Not all have the composure
Now there are two kinds of criticism,
The positive and the negative, which comes to us in
All forms and fashions
In your home, in your workplace, in your church, in the
Market place
Criticism, Criticism, Criticism.
Which is good or bad, within its contexts
They who live good shall suffer criticism
And I do not want to sound like I'm preaching
So I've been criticized for my silence
But that is just me,
I am a quiet person
I will speak when spoken to
When I am criticized for doing wrong
I will take it as a man
But why should I be criticized for doing that
Which is right?
I wish I could understand
But life is unfair at times
And it's up to the person whose
Life has meaning, to allow criticism to either build
Him or break him
Which one is it?
And if he or she is what they claim to be
One with integrity, who lives morally
And if they are criticized for this,
Then they are doing something good.
Some people criticize you for no reason at all
It doesn't necessarily mean you are at fault
They are just mean, and you with the character
That special nature, will not even bother with their
Criticism, for you are bigger than that.

And if you are living without criticism
Check yourself out, maybe you are dead
And it really doesn't matter
But once you are living, look out for criticism
And if you must be a critic, be to the upliftment
And maybe, we will see progress in our homes, in our work places
In our communities, in our churches, and the world we live in will be a better place.

Words Got Power

You know the power of words and the cliché that says
Sticks and stones may break my bones
But words can do me nothing
If that is true
Why do you take offence in words like these?
You're stupid, you're foolish, you're no good
And so on, and so on.
What are you then a hypocrite?
You said words can do me nothing.
As a child growing up, those words I hated to pronounce
It's the reason I amounted to nothing
Words that cause a still growth
Words that cost me my marriage
Words that have me in bondage
So it's not the stick and stones that did the damage
But the words, words of life and death
Words that spoke nothing good to me
And you would not believe how many at times I tried
To take my life
Probably I did in my mind
But I did not have the guts to go ahead with it.
To be another statistic
One who might have fallen through the cracks
Power of life and death is in the tongue
So watch your words, they are powerful.

Utopia

For my entire life, I believed that there's a place
Other than earth where we will have true happiness
Not in the planets which are in our universe
For even that would be folded up like a vesture
And my hope is not there, but in a promise.
I have been called a fool to believe in a promise
Because Utopia is imaginary, but heaven is real
It's got mansions there, but on earth we got
Mansions too. So why then you are not living in one?
And if you are living in one, how come you are not happy?
Two thousand years ago, a great man once said
Where He is, we will be there also
And that's a promise worth believing
For this world is full of conflicts
And you do not know who will push that button,
And cause a nuclear holocaust
So we do not need a false hope as Utopia
But a promise where heaven will be our home.
Where it will be perfect, so believe, and not in
Utopia.

Why Don't You Curse God and Die?

Wow! The madness of some people
Saying things they ought not to say, Ouch!
Knowing the tongue is a powerful muscle.
For I heard their choice words
Which only spells their destruction
And God is not a man that he should lie
And no one wants to hear that.
Their pain blinds them, so they are lashing out
Hating him, "God", without a cause
And the devil "instigator" in the background
Saying that's good
Job's wife said to him, why don't you curse God
And die of what he was going through at the time?
Pain and sufferings and headaches, the loss of all
His children, but he, "Job", chose his words carefully
He replied. You foolish woman, be angry and sin not
Why don't you curse God and die?
Does that make any sense?
You'll just be putting yourself in harm's way
For the same God you think of cursing
Will be your judge at the end.

This Generation

No one understood me because of the stand I took
I am a godly man and that's final
When others are compromising
Not seeing what's coming after
Destruction on them, who do such things
Living their lives outside the commandments
The fool said there is no God, but I am not taking
the chance to believe that.
For who created the universe and its planets,
the cosmos, and the milky way
I know it was not me, and I take no glory
For any work I did not do, but for my poems, oh yeah.
They said I will amount to nothing
Are they pulling my strings? I am no man's puppet
I was created to give God praise
And live according to his ways
That's why they do not understand me.
I am unusual, royal, a generation chosen
And no, I am not mad.
Special, if you asked me
For I meant it, and I understand me
And I'll live accordingly to the beliefs
Which were there at the beginning
Who understands me is God
Possibly my wife, and it's okay
I am happy and yet sad at the same time
Four hundred years I've been saying it
It's coming, the rain, but they are not taking me on
They love the way they are living
And I am in the middle of this generation
Who am I?
I am Noah.

Swastika

Yes, the haughty life style of some
And when they will get off from that high horse.
For they think that they are all that
Separating themselves by a symbol.
A symbol of hate, swastika.
And who would have thought that the cross
Could be twisted like that
But it's not for the right reason.
For the cross symbolizes hope, love and joy
But to these people who cannot embrace forgiveness,
Is the cross adopted for racist purposes
And love has its cross, and hate has its cross, too.
Which is, swastika.

They Are Here

Yes, my day went well until it was time to sleep
I went to bed, and this is what I dreamt.
It's a little bit sketchy, but I'll do my best to tell it
It was late in the night, Trinidad time (2:00 am)
My head on my pillow, tossing and turning as the dream unfolds
Men, all in white, on a plane that landed there
At the Piarco International Airport
Trinidad, of all places.
I look, I gaze at these men who were all in white apparel,
Showing that they are clean as they "Disembark from the plane"
But little did we know, that these men came for a reason
Peace,
They speak with a tone under their breath
But on their thighs were explosives
They are here, these terrorists
And Trinidad, a safe haven.

From Fiction to Reality

Life presents us with so much drama
Human beings alone with their day to day dogma
Who needs fiction that I might write their stories
Instead
True events with a little humour
That I put pen to paper
And write what's in front of me
The cries, do animation feel pain? Question
But we need fictions, cartoons for a better word
or the children's sake
Because they are too much in big people business
Where is the parental control
From fiction to reality?
Who's speeding up their growth? Questions
Oh, it's the age we are living in
Where everything is moving at a speed
As if the finish line is racing towards us
That it should be the other way around
The days shortened for the elect's sake
So fiction wants reality before it's too late
Moving away from imagination
Children making children
Something meant for big people (married)
From fiction to reality, an unwanted pregnancy
Racing hormones in a six years old
The world's game all over, and over again
Did you not read it in my first book?
Streams of poetic proverbs
Is that religion?
No, of course not
And that's beside the point
Let me put it to you straight
Game of Thrones,
Wheat and tares must grow together
Until harvested

There is one book that explains it all
And you will see that I was right all along
From fiction to reality, that it was no make-believe
Unless you're blind, not seeing
What's happening around you
It's just a matter of time death comes knocking
And nobody is ready for that
When I came to an understanding
Death is something everybody is trying to avoid
With their plastic surgeries
But, but, time will not go back two years for you
It still remains committed to carry you to your maker
From fiction to reality, there is no escaping it
It's life, and why it is this way?
In closing, I think enough has been said
From fiction to reality, my turn to run this race
So I'll see you all on the other side.

Verily, Verily, I Say

Come on, come on, look at the mess you made
It seems we are people that make a mess of things
Yeah, when we take things into our own hands
What do you expect?
Tampering with things we ought not to, why?
All in the name of science, one proclaims
Subjecting the whole human race to their faith
Did I vote of becoming a guinea pig? No
And now I am fighting for my life in this place
Verily, verily, I say, somebody got to pay
For this novel 19 Corona virus was not of my doing
And I am paying for their mistake
Where is the love for us humans
Or, collateral damage, another weapon in their arsenal?
This man of sin is already evident
As everything falls into place
Verily, verily, I say, what a day to be humans.

Made in the USA
Monee, IL
03 May 2026